Foreward

I have written 2 books about a sport close to my heart. This book is a deviation from the normal; it feels like writing my first paperback again. Some days I get bored, and on some days, when I find myself in a new place, my objective is to hunt information, no matter how useless, obscure, pointless, or irrelevant.

Few of these facts are relevant to me; for example, I play a part in facts 98 & 405 in this book, and no, I will not give you the page numbers.

I'd like to briefly point out that these facts were accurate as they were presented to me at the time of writing (circa late December 2022). I have obtained facts from various sources before their respective inclusions.

I hope you find these fascinating, and if not, I'm sure all 500 of these facts will annoy people in some fashion.

500 Useless Facts That Nobody Wanted To Know

1. The study of oceans on celestial bodies other than earth is known as "exo-oceanography".

2. The most common given name in the world is "Mohammed".

3. In 2015, the White House lifted a ban on taking selfies.

4. When referring to tyre sizes, the first number refers to the width of the tyre in millimetres.

5. When he was mummified, King Tutankhamun had an erect penis.

6. It costs the U.S. government more than 1 cent for every 1 cent coin that is minted.

7. When Valery Giscard d'Estaing was the president of France, he slowed down the tempo of the national anthem.

8. The two termini of the Jubilee Line on the London Underground are Stanmore and Stratford.

9. Cars in the UK that have a registration plate with a Union Jack on a green background, are electric vehicles.

10. Frenchman Boris Vian wrote several novels under the pseudonym "Vernon Sullivan".

11. Ville-d'Avray is situated in Ile-de-France.

12. Yerevan, the capital of Armenia was settled as early as 3,300 BCE.

13. CMN is the IATA code for Mohammed V International Airport in Casablanca, Morocco.

14. Bagels originated in Poland but there is some evidence that they were first made in modern day Germany.

15. The Monument to the Great Fire of London is 62 metres (202 feet) in height.

16. Most of the land owned by the Duchy of Cornwall is outside of Cornwall.

17. The Sercquiais language native to Sark, only has 3 native speakers as of 2022.

18. Broccoli comes from the Latin word "Brachium" meaning arm or branch.

19. The Windows 98 operating system had its mainstream support discontinued on 30th June 2002.

20. In a 2014 Harvard study by Joshua Goodman, left handed people earn 9-19% less than their right handed peers.

21. Bangladesh is the only UN recognised country that ends in the letter H.

22. The indentation or depression often found in bricks is called a "Frog".

23. In Western Australia, it's illegal to possess more than 50kg of potatoes.

24. On the 16th December 2022 in Swanage, Dorset; it was 3 degrees centigrade (37 Fahrenheit).

25. Australia has the largest population of feral camels in the world.

26. Muntjac is a variety of deer.

27. The splendid poison frog became extinct in 2020.

28. The Electric Light Orchestra's "Time" album reached number one in West Germany.

29. The winner of the 2005 Crufts' Best in Show award was a Norfolk Terrier named "Cracknor Cause Celebre".

30. The average dentist salary in Spain during 2022, was 6,570 EUR per month.

31. Dolphins sleep with one eye open.

32. The Republic of Turkey was proclaimed on the 29th October 1923.

33. Colombian goalkeeper René Higuita appeared in 68 games for his country and scored 3 goals.

34. The maximum score in a game of cribbage is 29.

35. King Christian X of Denmark was also the last king of Iceland.

36. Citizens of the Vatican City do not pay taxes.

37. Creme Puff was recorded as the longest living cat, she lived for 38 years and 3 days.

38. Soilwork is a Swedish death metal band that was formerly known as Inferior Breed until 1996.

39. "Prisencolinensinainciusol" is a 1972 song by Adriano Celentano, the song and lyrics are made up and are gibberish but intended to sound like English with an American accent.

40. A goat has 189 bones.

41. The Vatican City's flag does not have a defined proportion, some flags use a square flag with the Yellow and White colours of the flag and some flag use the same ratio as the Italian flag.

42. Two of William Shakespeare's plays have been translated into Klingon.

43. La Gaîté Lyrique in the 3rd arrondissement of Paris, has a total of 9,500 square metres

of floor space, its large hall has a capacity of 308 seated.

44. The Our Lady of Coromoto Church was founded in 1951 in Punto Fijo, Venezuela; the church was elevated to the status of Cathedral in 1997.

45. Track 7 on To Rococo Rot's 2004 album Hotel Morgan is titled "Plong" and is 18 seconds long.

46. The 13th word of the 13th chapter in Ian Fleming's "Live And Let Die" is expect.

47. The fine for failing to wear a seatbelt in the front or rear seat of a car in Austria, is 35 EUR.

48. The Reliant Rialto was a three wheeled car in production from 1982 to 1998.

49. ABC1 was a former television channel available in the UK & Ireland, the channel included programming from the American network of the same name, it was in service from 2004 to 2007.

50. The dots above the lower case letters i and j are known as "Tittles".

51. The shortest sentence in the English language is: "Go."

52. The most expensive optional extra on a car, is a Breitling clock for the Bentley Bentayga, the price tag comes in at 230,000 USD.

53. Andorra FC are a football team that play in the Spanish football league system despite being based in Andorra, not Spain.

54. Berwick Rangers are another example of the above, are a football team based in England, however play in the Scottish football league system.

55. The worst example of the above is that New Zealand based football team Wellington Phoenix, play in the Australian domestic top division.

56. The name of the hot beverage Caffé mocha, is derived from the city of Mocha in Yemen.

57. Owners of Ferraris who do not follow the contractual terms, can be banned from buying any Ferrari; examples of blacklisted individuals include Justin Bieber and Nicholas Cage.

58. On the 12th February 1986, near Musina, South Africa; an anti-tank mine is detonated by a pick-up truck; no-one was injured.

59. In 2004, Jeanna Giese from Wisconsin became the first known survivor of rabies.

60. Cabbages are a rich source in Vitamins C & K.

61. The number of possible chess games are greater than number of atoms in the universe.

62. King William II of England had no wives or children, and is speculated that he may have been homosexual.

63. The international calling code for Madagascar is +261.

64. The average price for a Cappuccino in Quezon City, Philippines in 2022; was 151 Philippine Pesos.

65. The world's largest producer of Aluminium is The People's Republic of China.

66. The world's largest producer of Aluminium Foil is Germany.

67. The most popular name for a baby girl in Finland for Finnish speakers in 2004 was: "Emma".

68. The most popular name for a baby girl in Finland for Swedish speakers in 2004 was also: "Emma".

69. "Yesterday" from the Beatles is the most covered song of all time.

70. A "419 scam" is known as such as section 419 of the Nigerian Criminal Code refers to fraud.

71. In 2011, the Television licence was abolished in Singapore.

72. In 2021, the cost for renewing a driving licence in Egypt was 55 Egyptian Pounds.

73. The standard font used for road signage in Italy is known as "Alfabeto Normale".

74. Peaches were once known as "Persian Apples".

75. On March 4th, 1975; Iran signed a trade deal pledging to spend 22 billion dollars in the U.S. over a ten year period.

76. "Qabeli Palaw" is a rice dish from Afghanistan, it consists of pilau rice with raisins, carrots, and beef or lamb.

77. "Varroa destructor" is a species of parasitic mite that causes varroosis among honey bees.

78. Milija Mrdak was the coach of the Serbian team during the 2012 FIVB Volleyball World League.

79. 456 Montgomery Plaza in San Francisco, California has 26 floors.

80. The ZIP code of the Netflix Corporate Headquarters in Los Gatos, California is 95032.

81. In 2001, during an episode of British game-show "Fifteen to One", the host William G. Stewart gave a lengthy presentation on why the Elgin Marbles should be returned to Greece, the broadcaster was later criticised for the stunt.

82. Wilhelm Gallhof who died in 1918, was once one of Germany's most prominent painters of nude women.

83. Since 2005, dual nationality is allowed in Armenia.

84. In the U.S. state of Montana, you are allowed to own a pet Lion.

85. The most expensive Pokémon card ever sold was a Pikachu Illustrator that sold for 5.275 million USD in 2021.

86. Wireless signal strength is measured in decibel milliwatts.

87. Eddie Slovik was executed by the U.S. Army for desertion during the Second World War.

88. Estel Ashworth was granted a presidential pardon by Bill Clinton on Christmas Eve 1998, for the offence of "theft of mail by a postal employee" in 1974.

89. TV Presenter James May's star sign is Capricorn.

90. Bananas are a distant relative of ginger, turmeric, and cardamom.

91. Dame Vanessa Redgrave declined a damehood in 1999, but accepted it in 2022.

92. The most viewed website in Turkmenistan in 2020, was Google.

93. The most expensive camera ever sold was a Leica 0-series no. 105 that sold for 15 million USD in 2022.

94. Bhutan is the world's only carbon-sink country, meaning it absorbs more carbon dioxide than it produces.

95. "Wiki" is Hawaiian for Quick.

96. Saudi Arabia and Iran are the only remaining countries that enforce the death penalty for sorcery and witchcraft.

97. The Activity Toy of the Year in 2009 was the "Crayola Color Wonder Magic Brush".

98. In 2019, over 24 million passengers travelled through Berlin's Tegel Airport.

99. In the first quarter of 2021, Vivo was the mobile phone manufacturer with the 3rd largest market share in India.

100. The M96 is a motorway with no public highway access on the grounds of the Fire Service College in Moreton-in-Marsh, Gloucestershire; it's listed as a mock motorway but fully equipped with emergency phones, cats eyes, speed cameras, and road signs.

101. Eric Bristow won the 1980 Embassy World Darts Championship.

102. Disqualified driver codes BA10 and BA30 stay on your driving record for 4 years in Great Britain.

103. At the end of 2016, there were 124 Citroen C3 Pluriel Kiwi's licensed on British roads.

104. The fifth most popular language studied on Duolingo in 2020, was Italian.

105. The 18th most common password according to Reader's Digest in 2022 was: "Qwertyuiop".

106. The unhyphenated form of the word "ashtray" didn't experience casual usage until 1926.

107. The kakapo, is the world's fattest parrot with a top speed of around 5 miles per hour.

108. The sixth track on Automatic Man's début album released in 1976 is "Geni Geni".

109. "Griffonage" is an alternative name for unintelligible handwriting.

110. In Scotland, it is illegal to be drunk and in charge of a cow.

111. The world's shortest flight is between Westray and Papa Westray in the Orkney Islands; the record time for this flight is 53 seconds.

112. West Covina in California is home to a museum devoted to shoehorns.

113. In 2022, the UK's most popular ice cream flavour was Vanilla.

114. In the same survey, the 7th most popular flavour was Pistachio.

115. The second-highest score in the British game-show Countdown, was 148; set by Stu Harkness on 24th November 2021.

116. "Gingertat" is an anagram of "Targeting".

117. The winning ticket of the first EuroMillions draw, was purchased in France.

118. The machine used for the first National Lottery draw in 1994, was named "Guinevere".

119. Caterpillars only have six legs.

120. Strofilas in Greece is Europe's oldest city.

121. Salt Bae's real name is "Nusret Gökçe".

122. Port Huron in Michigan was incorporated in 1857.

123. The water chestnut is not a nut, but a tuber.

124. The final episode of Frasier was watched by 33.7 million people.

125. The 3rd most ordered beverage in U.S. Starbucks stores in 2021, was the Pumpkin Spice Latte.

126. A Mars Bar contains 230 calories.

127. The average height for an Austrian male is 179cm.

128. The standard rate of Income Tax in the Republic of Ireland is 20%.

129. "Good cause" is a legal term often used in the U.S. to denote adequate grounds for performing or failing to perform an action, this concept is often determined on a case by case basis.

130. Judge Judy Sheindlin has also been a prosecutor as well as a family court judge.

131. "Anorak" is a word that comes from the Greenlandic language.

132. Americium has the atomic number 95.

133. An adult weighing 70kg has approximately 0.2 milligrams of Gold in their body, which according to market rates on the 23rd December 2022, is worth 1 U.S. penny.

134. In 2009, the Independent State of Samoa changed the side of the road of which cars are driven, Samoa used to drive on the right, but now they drive on the left.

135. The average time for men to fall in love is 88 days.

136. The average time for women to fall in love is 134 days.

137. It takes just over 7 days for Ganymede to orbit Jupiter.

138. The Chinese company Yutong is the world's largest producer of Buses.

139.   The Sun Protection Factor (SPF) on a sunblock will only give you indication on how well it protects you from UVB rays.

140.   The Pharaohs of Ancient Egypt were buried with onions.

141.   In the U.S., the most popular month for a mother to give birth, is August.

142.   The last person to be executed by guillotine in Switzerland, was Hans Vollenweider.

143.   The majority of the world's footballs come from Sialkot, Pakistan.

144.   Intaglio is any printmaking technique where an image is cut into a surface; etching and engraving are examples of this.

145.   Shoe sizes in the U.S. and the UK are measured in a unit called a "barleycorn" which is one third of an inch. Someone who wears Size 10 shoes is a barleycorn bigger than someone who wears Size 9 shoes.

146.   The average human has 10 pints of blood, roughly a tenth of their body weight.

147. A person uses on average 20,000 sheets of toilet paper per year.

148. In 2021, a survey revealed that the most likely people to use swear words online, were French.

149. The average IQ for the Netherlands is 100.

150. In 1971, the life expectancy in Mali was 33 years.

151. 58% of school pupils who are bullied on a daily basis, have experienced the death of a relative.

152. When Lady Sarah McCorquodale dated then Prince Charles, she introduced him to her sister, who would later become Diana, Princess of Wales.

153. The highest temperature ever recorded in Hungary, was 41.9 degrees centigrade on the 20th July 2007.

154. The state beverage of the U.S. state of Indiana, is water.

155. Cannibal Holocaust was a 1980 Italian Horror film that was so controversial that the director was charged with murder, the actors had to appear in court to prove that they were alive.

156. The letter A is not present in any number between 0 and 999.

157. The 3rd largest city in Burkina Faso by population is Koudougou.

158. The 3rd largest city by area in California, is California City which only had a population of 14,973 in the 2020 census.

159. Despite its name, Milk of Magnesia doesn't contain milk.

160. Tenderstem Broccoli is a hybrid of broccoli and Chinese kale and was first cultivated in Japan in the 1990s.

161. Jelly in the USA, is known as Jam in the UK; and Jelly in the UK, is known as Jell-O in the USA.

162. In February 2020, British comedian Joe Lycett changed his name by deed poll to

"Hugo Boss" to protest the company's use of cease and desist letters to small businesses, Mr. Boss changed his name back to Joe Lycett 2 months later.

163.   In Thailand, it is illegal to drive topless.

164.   The winner of Series 46 of the the UK game show Countdown, was Ben Wilson.

165.   In July 2022, American athlete Devon Allen was disqualified at the World Athletic Championships because he started 1 thousandth of a second too soon.

166.   St Walpurga or Walburga was a missionary who received a notice to pay her German TV licence fee in 2003, she died in the 8th century.

167.   The Toledo, Peoria, and Western Railway is a short line railway that began operation in 1863 that runs from Mapleton, Illinois to Logansport, Indiana.

168.   "Habibi Oud" is a 2001 Arabic pop single from Lebanese singer Amal Hijazi

that has a run time of 4 minutes and 2 seconds.

169. Cape Leblond is a cape that forms the northern section of Lavoisier Island in Antarctica, which is known in Chile as Serrano and in Argentina, Mitre.

170. Minor planets 48848 to 48852, were all discovered on my birthday; 20th March 1998.

171. In the Summer Olympic games, Yugoslavia took home the gold medal for Water Polo in 1968, 1984, and 1988.

172. Charles Downing Lay was an American landscape architect born in 1877, he won the Silver medal at the 1936 Olympic Games for Town Planning.

173. Cricket was played for the only time in the Olympic Games in 1900, Great Britain won against France; Britain won by 158 runs and the French team composed mostly of British expats living in France.

174. A leap year is only a leap year if it can be divided by 4, but if it's a century year, it must be divisible by 400; for example, 1900 was not a leap year but 2000 was; the next leap year to take place with a -00 suffix won't occur until 2400.

175.   Briarfield Academy in Northern Louisiana was founded as a segregated school in 1970, the school won the LISA football championships in 1979, 1989, and 1991.

176.   In the men's FIFA World Cup, a hat-trick has only been scored in the final twice. Geoff Hurst in the 1966 Final where England won against West Germany, and Kylian Mbappé in the 2022 Final where France lost to Argentina on a penalty shoot out.

177.   The first generation Opel Omega was a model of executive car that was in production from 1986-1994, it is known as a Chevrolet Omega in Brazil, Holden Commodore in Australia & New Zealand, and a Vauxhall Carlton in the UK.

178.   There are 7 emirates that make up the country of the United Arab Emirates, the ruler of the Emirate of Abu Dhabi also serves as the national head of state.

179. Someone who was born when the first flight by the Wright Brothers took place in 1903, would have only been 65 when the Apollo 11 moon landing occurred.

180. American writer Robert Bloch, outlived the Soviet Union.

181. Liam Silcocks stood in the South West Wiltshire constituency of the UK 2017 general election as an independent candidate, he finished last with 590 votes.

182. Breadcrumb navigation is used as an aid to navigation in user interfaces within computers, it is a reference to the trail of breadcrumbs in Hansel and Gretel.

183. Klik is an Israeli brand of confectionery that in 2011, was Israel's second leading confectionery brand.

184. The first iPhone that launched in 2007, only sold 6.1 million units; compared to the first iPad that was released in 2010 sold 15 million units.

185.   Wikipedia has been blocked in Myanmar since February 2021.

186.   Born James Bradford in 1954, Jimmy Nail adopted his stage name from when he worked in a glass factory and stood on a spike.

187.   The best result achieved by South Korean tennis player Kwon Soon-woo at the Wimbledon Singles, was the Second Round in 2021.

188.   Pinehurst F.C. was an association football club that played in the Hellenic Football League from 1966 to 1978. The team won the Hellenic League Division One title in their first year, and remained in the same division until the team left the league in 1978.

189.   "Loose" is a song by S1mba featuring KSI, it reached a peak of number 7, on the New Zealand Singles Chart.

190.   Chile is the world's largest copper producer.

191.   For a donation of 150,000 USD, you can buy citizenship of the Caribbean nation of Saint Kitts and Nevis.

192.   The first modern land mine was first engineered by General Gabriel J Rains.

193.   Ketchup was originally prepared with mushrooms instead of tomatoes.

194.   In Portugal you're forbidden from naming your newborn baby Charlotte or Tom.

195.   The word "Scrabble" scores 14 points in a game of Scrabble.

196.   The Wolf of Wall Street set a world record for the most swear words in a film, the F-word is used 506 times.

197.   Before his execution in 2011, Lawrence Brewer's last meal request was two chicken fried steaks with gravy and sliced onions; a triple patty bacon cheeseburger; a cheese omlette with ground beef, tomatoes, onions, bell peppers, and jalapenos; a bowl of fried okra with ketchup; one pound of barbecue meat with half a loaf

of white bread; three fully loaded fajitas; a meat-lover's pizza; one pint of vanilla ice cream; a slab of peanut butter fudge with crushed peanuts on top; and three root beers. Brewer told officials he wasn't hungry and refused to eat any of it, prompting Texas to abolish the practice.

198.   Sonny and his Wild Crows are a rockabilly band from Budapest, Hungary; Sonny is on vocals & guitar, Crazy Benny plays the piano, Gordon Taylor is on bass, and Little Tommy hits the drums.

199.   Désirée by Annemarie Selinko topped the New York Times Fiction Best Seller list for 31 consecutive weeks in 1953.

200.   In the Mortal Kombat video game series, Charred Mountain in Earthrealm is the base of the Red Dragon clan.

201.   As of September 2022, travelling from Calais to Troyes on French motorways, will cost 37 EUR in tolls.

202.   When referring to pencils, HB stands for "hard black".

203. Henryk Magnuski and Al Gross are credited with inventing the walkie-talkie.

204. The first inexpensive celluloid sunglasses were invented in 1929 by Sam Foster.

205. The 10,000 Bruneian Dollar note is the highest valuable banknote still in circulation, as of 21st December 2022, it is worth 7,397 USD.

206. 161 multiplied by 23 is 3,703.

207. In March 2022, 13-year old Jiya Rai, swam 29 kilometres across the Palk Strait that connects India and Sri Lanka in 13 hours and 10 minutes.

208. The KF01108 is a model of Shatter-resistant ruler made by Belgian firm, Q-Connect.

209. There are 2 Australian states named after Queen Victoria, Victoria and Queensland.

210. The "Dictionnaire historique et critique" by Pierre Bayle was translated into

English in 1710 by Pierre des Maizeaux as "An Historical and Critical Dictionary".

211. Sir Joseph Paxton was the member of parliament of Coventry from 1854 until his death in 1865; he was the first cultivator of the Cavendish Banana, the most consumed type of banana in the world.

212. The 1970 Omani coup d'état saw the Sultan of Oman's depose his father and rule the country until his death in 2020; both sides of the coup each only had 1 wounded.

213. The 15th letter of the Hebrew alphabet is Samekh.

214. "Tachwedd" in Welsh language translates to November, which literally means "slaughtering" which refers to the time when livestock and animals are killed before winter.

215. "The Giant Spoon" is a 15 feet tall stainless steel structure near the town of Cramlington, England; it was designed by the artist Bob Budd, it is not accessible by road.

216. Phenylalanine hydroxylase also known as PAH is an enzyme based in Chromosome 12 of Human DNA.

217. A lady-in-waiting is a female assistant at a royal court, these women were nobles in their own right but would tend to a noblewoman a rank above themselves, they are considered more of a courtier or companion rather than a servant.

218. The father of Al Gore, Al Gore Sr. was first elected as senator for Tennessee in 1952.

219. Sloths are colourblind.

220. Damoiseau is a sugarcane juice rum based in Guadeloupe.

221. The Stockport Garrick Theatre which opened on 24th October 1901, it's described as the oldest "little theatre" in the United Kingdom, which is an amateur theatre that has full control over its premises.

222. Naomi is Ruth's mother-in-law in the Book of Ruth.

223.   "Ecce Homo" is Latin for "behold the man".

224.   Hieronymus Bosch born Jheronimus Van Aken in the Dutch city of 's-Hertogenbosch, created 2 paintings titled "Ecce Homo" both paintings are estimated to have been painted 40 years apart.

225.   "Ecce Homo" are the opening words to the theme song of the TV series Mr. Bean.

226.   Acarapis woodi is a parasite that affects honey bees, it was first observed on the Isle of Wight at the start of the 20th century.

227.   Menheniot Rail Station is 262 miles from London Paddington via Bristol Temple Meads, and according to the Office of Rail and Road; the station had 1,924 passengers in the 2021/22 year.

228.   Parallax SX is a model of discontinued micro-controller, there are known issues with the SX key software if you operate on a Windows Vista.

229. In a South African poll in 2021, the 3rd worst version of Microsoft Windows, was Windows Vista.

230. In the same poll, the 3rd best version of Microsoft Windows, was Windows XP.

231. "Bliss" is the title of the image used as the default Windows XP wallpaper, Charles O'Rear took the picture in 1996, Microsoft bought the rights to the image in 2000 and is considered a contender for the most viewed photograph in history.

232. Langsett Reservoir in South Yorkshire supplies water to the populations of Sheffield and Barnsley, one of the farms that was abandoned included "North America Farm" and the ruins of the farm are still standing near the reservoir and during the Second World War, the ruins were used for target practice by Allied soldiers.

233. In 2015, Italian chef Gennaro 'Gino' D'Acampo legally changed his name to "Gennaro Sheffield D'Acampo" on the UK panel show, Celebrity Juice.

234. 37% of the world population have O+ blood.

235. North Korea only has 4 television channels.

236. The Number 1 pin on Apple's Lightning connector cable, is Ground.

237. The Taim Ecological Station in Rio Grande do Sul, Brazil was designated as Ramsar Wetland on 22nd March 2017.

238. Birds don't urinate.

239. The device used to fasten a scarf or neckerchief, is called a woggle.

240. The most expensive vinyl record ever sold on Discogs.com was a 12 inch promotional single from British DJ Scaramanga Silk entitled "Choose Your Weapon", only 20 copies of the vinyl have been made.

241. The town of Buford, Wyoming was auctioned in 2012; a year later, the site was re-branded as "PhinDeli Town Buford" as the new owners of the town sold PhinDeli coffee, a coffee brand from Vietnam.

242. "Nguyen" is Vietnam's most common surname.

243. Vietnamese is a recognised minority language in the Czech Republic.

244. In Floorball, there are 6 players plus a goalkeeper on a team.

245. Mall walking is a pastime in which people walk or jog through the indoor areas of shopping malls; it is popular within the U.S.

246. The earliest recorded use of the '@' symbol was in a Bulgarian translation of a Greek text written in 1345.

247. "Mummerset" is a fictitious dialect of English used by actors to represent a stereotypical West Country accent, it is a portmanteau of Mummer, an archaic term for a folk actor and Somerset, a large rural county in South West England.

248.   A poll in 2019 revealed that the UK's worst rail station among the busiest 100, was London Earlsfield.

249.   In the UK, chocolate covered cakes are sold without any value added tax; but chocolate covered biscuits are liable to a value added tax rate of 20%.

250.   In 1991, the Jaffa Cake was the basis of a tribunal to determine if the Jaffa Cake was a cake or biscuit for tax purposes; the court found that the tasty treat was a cake and therefore can be consumed tax free.

251.   The world's shortest poem is credited to Aram Saroyan, it comprises of the lower-case letter 'm' with 4 legs.

252.   Blu Tack was invented by Alan Holloway that was intent on being used as a sealant, the product was pliable and elastic, Blu Tack was not always blue, it was originally white.

253.   The B-side to Marcus Marr's 2015 single "Brown Sauce" is titled

"Peacemakers" and has a tempo of 112 BPM.

254.   At the end of the 1991 FA Charity Shield match, Arsenal and Tottenham Hotspur finished the match with a goalless draw; the shield was shared and this was the last time the shield was shared.

255.   "Mi Tzu" which in Chinese translates to "rice ancestor", is a Northern Chinese martial art that utilises fast, and long-ranged movements; similar to the Zha Chuan style of Long Fist.

256.   Babies have the ability to understand sound and can differentiate noises while inside the womb.

257.   The world record for the most rubber bands stretched over a face in a minute, is held by Shripad Krishnarao Vaidya who managed to stretch 82 bands over his face.

258.   An LR06 battery is the same as a AA battery.

259. According to a survey in 2021, the most commonly gifted item for Christmas, was bars of candy & chocolate.

260. In the same survey, home-made gifts came second.

261. In the year 1990, the board game Mouse Trap had a retail price of £12.25.

262. £100 in 1962 would be worth £1,711.86 in November 2022 according to the average Bank of England inflation rates.

263. Ferrari Challenge was a racing video game released on the Playstation 3, on the 4th July 2008 in Europe.

264. The last game to be released on the Playstation 3, was Shakedown: Hawaii; released on the 20th August 2020.

265. "Das Mirakel" is a 1912 silent film from Germany, it was directed by Romanian Mime Misu, the feature's length is 4,000 feet of film.

266. "The Right To Be Happy" is a 1916 silent film released on Christmas Day, distributed by Universal Pictures and starred New Zealand born actor Rupert Julian as Ebeneezer Scrooge.

267. The sixth series of the children's TV series "Arthur" has 10 episodes.

268. "No. 5" painted in 1948 by American artist Jackson Pollock, sold for 140 million USD in 2006.

269. 33 squared is 1,089.

270. Usually in the UK, GCSE results are released on a Thursday but in 2010 they were instead released on a Tuesday.

271. Bauxite is primarily an ore of Aluminium but also contains small amounts of Gallium.

272. After the 1513 Battle of the Spurs, the victory for England & the Holy Roman Empire resulted in the Belgian town of Tournai captured by King Henry VIII, this made Tournai the only Belgian city to be ruled by England.

273.   The Class 624 trains operated by Deutsche Bahn were powered by an on-board diesel engine, the maximum speed of these locomotives is 75mph.

274.   In 2019, the Chinese spacecraft Chang'e 4, took cotton seeds to the far side of the moon.

275.   Autoeca, also known as Auto Tecnica Colombiana is the first motorcycle assembler in Colombia, the company is based in Colombia's second largest city, Medellín.

276.   One of the proposed names for Canada, Borealia; comes from the Latin word "Borealis" meaning 'northern', it would have been directly compared to Australia as "Australis" in Latin, means 'southern'.

277.   Nettie Stevens was an American biologist who discovered the sex determinant X & Y chromosomes.

278.   In the U.S., citizens and residents are issued with a 9 digit "Social Security" number which is a unique identifier for the country's social welfare system.

279. The UK equivalent, known as a "National Insurance" number, is also a 9 digit number, however the last 2 digits determine the day of the week that social benefits are paid, if these digits are between 00-19, then state benefits are paid on a Monday; if the numbers end in 20-39, state benefits are paid on a Tuesday; and so on.

280. Often seen in academic papers, "et al" is Latin for 'and others'.

281. Not often seen in academic papers, "inter alia" is Latin for 'among other things'.

282. At 11:11am, on the 27th November 1944; a military accident at RAF Fauld in Staffordshire, England resulted in the UK's largest non-nuclear explosion, it is estimated around 70 people died from the blast and the aftermath which included floods.

283. The price of diesel per litre at the Shell Gatwick North filling station at 7:00am on the 22nd June 2022, was £1.959 per litre.

284. The American ice cream & desserts chain Baskin Robbins, has outlets in Uruguay & Zimbabwe.

285. "Almirante" is the highest rank in the Ecuadorian Navy.

286. Charlotte reigned as the Grand Duchess of Luxembourg from 1919 until her abdication in 1964.

287. Her grandfather was King Miguel I of Portugal, who reigned from 1828 to 1834.

288. "You keep on giving me the hold up" are the opening words to Basement Jaxx's 2001 single, Romeo.

289. Blue is the most popular Crayola crayon colour.

290. Cerise, is a deep pinkish colour with the hex code #DE3163.

291. John Paul Getty, had a net worth of 6 billion USD at the time of his death in 1976.

292. Vieux-Boulogne is an unpasteurised cheese made from cow's milk near

Boulogne-sur-Mer in France; in 2007, it was declared the world's smelliest cheese.

293. More than 99% of the volume of the gases during a fart, are odourless.

294. The Osborne Bull is a symbol often seen on hilltops and roadsides throughout Spain; as of 2022, there are 92 of these bulls installed.

295. In Lithuania, conscription was abolished in 2008; in 2015, it was re-established after the 2014 invasion of Ukraine.

296. In the 2004 Syria census, the village of Bashawi had 253 inhabitants.

297. G-BOAD is the registration of the Concorde aircraft that currently holds the record for the fastest London Heathrow-New York JFK crossing, completed in 2 hours, 52 minutes, and 59 seconds.

298. Pop artist Stuart Semple, was born in Bournemouth, Dorset on the 12th September 1980.

299. The average speaking speed, is 150 words per minute.

300. "Rhinorrhea" is the medical term for runny nose.

301. Diarrhoea caused by viruses are more likely to be watery, lacking blood and mucus; conversely, bacterial diarrhoea will be more likely to contain blood and mucus.

302. On the 27th June 1931, Galicia declared its independence from Spain.

303. On the 28th June 1931, the newly formed Galician Republic, rejoined Spain.

304. The Convention on the Elimination of all Forms of Discrimination Against Women, is an international treaty that was adopted by the United Nations General Assembly, it has been hailed as an international "bill of rights" for women; as of 2023, the U.S. has not ratified the treaty.

305. According to Article 30 of the Constitution of Mexico, people born on Mexican territory regardless of their parents' nationality, are Mexican citizens at birth.

306.   In Svalbard, you are legally required to carry a gun whenever you leave the town of Longyearbyen, this is due to the risk of being mauled by polar bears.

307.   Like Rome, the city of Edinburgh, Scotland also claims to be built on seven hills.

308.   Picacho Peak in Arizona is a tautological place name, which is a location with parts of the name that share similar meaning, in this case Picacho Peak is a double tautology as Picacho in Spanish means 'peak'; and the name Picacho Peak literally means, "peak peak".

309.   Another example of the above is Torpenhow Hill in Northumberland, England; Tor, Pen, and How all mean 'hill' in Old English, Old Welsh, and Old Norse; therefore Torpenhow Hill is a quadruple tautology as the name literally means, "hill hill hill hill".

310.   According to legend, "The Pink House" in Newbury, Massachusetts was built due to the terms of a divorce settlement, a man was required to build a house for his ex-wife, but because the wife didn't specify where house should be built, the man built the house upon a salt marsh.

311.   The Shwethalyaung Buddha statue in Bago, Myanmar is 55 meters long and 16 meters tall and is believed to have been built in the 10th century.

312.   The town of Câmpulung Moldovenesc in Romania, is home to a wooden spoon museum.

313.   Neutral Moresnet was a condominium that existed between 1816 and 1920, Dr. Wilhelm Molly made an effort to make Neutral Moresnet the world's first Esperanto speaking state.

314.   The 1987 World Esperanto Congress which took place in Warsaw, Poland; had 5,946 participants.

315.   A study determined that the majority of navel lint, also known as belly button fluff; is blue.

316. Fe, Fi, Fo, Fum, and Phooey were the names of five mice that travelled to the Moon in the Apollo 17 space mission; the four surviving mice from the space mission were all killed and dissected.

317. "Bananadine" is the name of a fictional psychoactive substance that is obtained from banana peels, the hoax recipe for its extraction was first published in 1967.

318. Mount Athos is a region of Greece that bans women and female animals from entering its territory.

319. During the 1990s, Greek journalist Malvina Karali entered the Mount Athos sanctuary by dressing as a man.

320. In Singapore, connecting to another person's Wi-Fi is considered hacking and the penalty is a fine of $10,000 SGD, 3 years in jail, or both.

321. The average price for a litre of milk in Krishnanagar, India in 2022; was 50 Indian Rupees.

322. The average price of a month's rent for a 1 bedroom apartment in Ankara, Turkey in 2022; is 5,240 Turkish Lira.

323. The last surviving widow of a veteran of the U.S. Civil War, died in 2020 at the age of 101.

324. If Prince William is eventually crowned King of England, he will become the first blood descendant of King Charles II to take the throne.

325. "This Way Please" is a 1937 American musical comedy film starring Betty Grable, it has a running time of 73 minutes.

326. Janet Horne was the last person to be executed for witchcraft in the British Isles, the execution took place in the year 1727.

327. Hanging was available as a method of execution for treason & piracy with violence in the UK, until its final abolition on the 30th September 1998.

328. The average human will consume just over 100,000 pints of water in a lifetime.

329. The multi-national company Google and the first episode of the international TV game-show "Who Wants To Be A Millionaire?" began on the 4th September 1998.

330. As of December 2022, the 4th largest political party in the UK is the Co-operative Party with 26 seats in the House of Commons.

331. The archbishops of Canterbury & York, as well as the bishops of Durham, London, and Winchester; automatically have a seat in the House of Lords.

332. Ducks are known to eat small rocks, grit, gravel, and sand.

333. The European version of the casino game Roulette has a single zero, but the American version of Roulette has the single zero, and the double zero.

334. In roulette, a "Street" is a bet is placed onto three consecutive numbers in a horizontal line, for example: 4, 5, and 6.

335. blackfridaydeathcount.com is a website that counts deaths and injuries as a result of Black Friday Shopping.

336. A typical 1.7 ounce bag of M&M's will contain on average, 56 individual M&Ms.

337. The gestation period for ferrets is usually six weeks.

338. Honey Badgers often raid beehives to search for bee larvae and honey as part of its diet.

339. The bite force exerted by an adult Nile crocodile has been shown to measure around 22 Kilo-newtons.

340. Herodotus was an ancient Greek historian and geographer who was the first writer to perform a systematic investigation of previous events of historical importance.

341. The original name of the settlement Halicarnassus, was "Zephyria"

342. "Every Little Helps" was a slogan created by an advertising agency for the retail supermarket chain Tesco, it has been their slogan since 1993.

343.   An Islamic mortgage is a financial product that complies with Sharia law, it's a type of mortgage without any financial interest charged as under Sharia law, charging interest is haram.

344.   A poll in 2019 revealed that 24% of Americans prefer their steaks and hamburgers cooked well done.

345.   In the same survey, 23% of Americans prefer their steaks and hamburgers cooked medium-rare.

346.   In the same survey, 2% of Republican Party voters preferred a burnt steak, compared to 1% of Democratic Party voters.

347.   In 2011, a study revealed that 90% of computer users don't know how to use the CTRL+F command.

348.   The CTRL+F command is a search bar tool used to search for text in a document or web page.

349. Hair Clipper Guard Sizes increase by one eighth of an inch, per guard number; for example, a Number 3 guard leaves the hair three eighths of an inch from the head, where as a Number 4 guard leaves the hair four eighths of an inch.

350. Simplified, four eighths equals one half.

351. William Tunstall-Pedoe found that April 11, 1954, was statistically the most boring day in history.

352. "Before Present" is a time scale used by archaeologists and geologists, it refers to the time period before nuclear weapons testing altered the presence of isotopes in the atmosphere, the present according to the time scale is the 1st January 1950.

353. Art Martinich is a former American Midfielder who earned 3 caps for the U.S. national football team in 1973.

354. If you sprinkle Salt to a pan or griddle, pancakes won't stick.

355.   In April 2022, a 6 inch garlic pizza bread side at the Domino's Pizza on London Road, Liverpool; was £4.99.

356.   The average daily circulation of newspapers in Pakistan fell from 9.9 million in 2007 to 6.1 million in 2008.

357.   Burglars use chalk marks on houses to indicate messages to other burglars about the contents and occupants of the property; for example, an open book symbol means the occupant is vulnerable, and a circle with a cross through it means there's nothing worth stealing; this code has been nicknamed: "The Da Pinchi Code".

358.   In laundry symbols, a pictogram with a square and three vertical lines, means that you should drip dry the clothing item.

359.   2 Diagonal lines in the top-left corner of laundry symbols means "in the shade"; for example, a square and three vertical lines with 2 diagonal lines in the top-left corner means you should drip dry the clothes in the shade.

360. "Flying Cloud" was a 1954 project by the U.S. Air Force to use high altitude balloons to deliver bombs and weapons to enemy targets; controlling the accuracy on the balloons was impractical and the project was abandoned the following year.

361. In the average 102g medium serving of McDonalds French Fries, there are 68 fries.

362. McDonalds' Chicken McNuggets come in 4 distinct shapes, the ball, the bell, the bone, and the boot.

363. According to a YouGov survey, the boot is the fans' favourite Chicken McNugget shape.

364. Max Factor cosmetics was founded in 1909 by Max Factor Sr. Full name, Maksymilian Faktorowicz.

365. Bangladesh is an anagram of bagel hands.

366. Most natural red-headed people have brown eyes.

367. The highest grossing film of 2006, was Pirates of the Caribbean: Dead Man's Chest.

368. The 2003 World Series of Poker was won by Chris Moneymaker.

369. Chris Moneymaker's autobiography: "Moneymaker: How an Amateur Poker Player Turned $40 into $2.5 Million at the World Series of Poker" was published in February 2005.

370. As of 2022, Norwegian poker player Annette Obrestad is the youngest recipient of a World Series of Poker bracelet.

371. Lynn Redgrave is the only person to have been nominated for an Emmy, Grammy, Oscar, and a Tony without winning any of them.

372. Marvin Hamlisch and Richard Rodgers are the only two people to have won an Emmy, Grammy, Oscar, Tony, and a Pulitzer Prize.

373. Kendrick Lamar's album "Damn" was the first musical work not in the jazz or classical genre to have won a Pulitzer Prize.

374.   In 2020, 55% of all foreign tourists arriving in Algeria were Tunisian.

375.   In the UK, the 01625 telephone code is for the town of Macclesfield, Cheshire.

376.   Fan death is an urban myth that originates from South Korea, the theory is that an electric fan operating in a room with no open windows will cause asphyxiation.

377.   Charles Ingram, the man who was infamous for his role in the coughing scandal in the UK version of hit game-show Who Wants To Be A Millionaire? lost 3 of his toes in 2010.

378.   The Turnip Prize is a parody arts award that satirizes the Turner Prize.

379.   The winners of the 2019 Turner Prize were Lawrence Abu Hamdan, Helen Cammock, Oscar Murillo, and Tai Shani; as they all requested to be considered as a single group and the prize was jointly awarded.

380.   The winner of the 2019 Turnip Prize was Fanny Scorcher for the work entitled

"Bush Fire Down Under" which was a pair of knickers with a burnt hole in the front.

381.   The record low temperature for the month of September in the city of Suzhou, China; was 11.7 degrees centigrade.

382.   David Hieatt co-founded the Hiut Denim company.

383.   The average lifespan of a car alternator is 7 years.

384.   The planet Uranus makes a complete orbit around the sun once every 84 years.

385.   A total solar eclipse will occur on the 2nd August 2027, it will be the first total solar eclipse to happen in Tunisia in the 21st century.

386.   The Bosch Universal Rotak 36-550 has been described as the best lawnmower of 2022.

387.   In Namibia, only 7% of roads are paved.

388.   Albania is the world's 105th largest consumer of electricity.

389. In 2001, Malaria was the 7th leading cause of death in developing countries.

390. Marie Provazníková was the first defector from the Olympic Games when she refused to return home to her native Czechoslovakia after the 1948 Olympics in London.

391. The transmitter of the former Atlantic 252 long wave radio station in the Republic of Ireland had once broadcast a long wave signal so strong that during the night, listeners could sometimes hear the radio station from Brazil.

392. The 17th amendment to the U.S. constitution allowed for the direct election of senators, prior to this Senators were appointed by the state legislatures.

393. Napoleon Bonaparte gave Jewish people in France full citizenship rights, something that was extremely progressive at the time in Europe.

394. Napoleon Bonaparte also wrote about the creation of a Jewish state and homeland in Israel.

395. Israel is the only country in the world to have had more trees today than it did since the start of the 20th century.

396. Commercial trading and sale of human organs is illegal in every country, except Iran.

397. The largest manufacturer of tyres in world, is Lego.

398. The last use of the guillotine as a form of capital punishment in France, was in 1977.

399. The world's longest paperclip chain created in 24 hours by an individual measured 5,340 meters and was constructed by Dan Meyer in 2004.

400. "Kissin Time" was the sixteenth studio album by British singer Marianne Faithfull.

401. David Bowie was left handed but opted to play most instruments with his right hand.

402. Bovril was invented by Scotsman John Lawson Johnston.

403. "Sayyid" meaning a Lord or Master is a surname for people who are direct descendants of the Islamic prophet Muhammad.

404. Most religious scholars agree that the first language of Jesus Christ was Aramaic.

405. Between April 2020 and March 2021, NHS England admitted 1,118 emergency patients because foreign objects were stuck in the ear.

406. In the same time period, only one patient was admitted to hospital because of "Other and unspecified effects of high altitude".

407. The Republic of Ireland accidentally made drugs such as ecstasy, ketamine, and crystal meth legal in 2015; The 1977 Misuse of Drugs Act was found unconstitutional by the Irish Court of Appeal because both houses of the Irish parliament had not agreed to the new additions, meaning that the drugs currently prohibited by the Act were technically still legal until the loophole closed the next day.

408. The first known Christmas card was sent to English King James I & his son Henry by Michael Maier in the year 1611.

409. King George II at the age of 60, was the last English king to lead troops into battle.

410. In the State of Texas, under the state's criminal code; duelling is legal as long if it only involves hand to hand combat.

411. Between 2016 and 2017, North Korean defectors shipped thousands of USB flash drives to the country; the information on the flash drives included news stories and information about the outside world, and also contained South Korean & Hollywood movies.

412.   A computer programmer named Jerry Jalava from Finland lost his finger in a motorcycle accident, after the crash he replaced his missing finger with a prosthetic replacement with a USB drive built in.

413.   At the time of his death, Richard Whiteley was believed to have been shown on British television for longer than anyone else alive, apart from Carole Hersee who was the girl on Test Card F.

414.   In 2011, the BBC reported that over 30 million calls were made to the UK's speaking clock.

415.   The UK's speaking clock telephone service was established in 1936 and demand normally peaks at 4 times of the year: 1am in the later stages of March & October when British Summer Time starts and ends, Just before midnight on New Years Eve, and just before 11am on Remembrance Sunday.

416.   "Moon Museum" is the name of an artwork that was left on the Moon during the Apollo 12 mission; on that artwork is a contribution by Andy Warhol who according to himself drew a stylized version of his initials which to the untrained eye can also be interpreted as a space rocket or a penis.

417.   When it comes to performing a baptism in Christianity, Methodists believe in the baptism of anyone regardless of age, whereas Baptists believe that baptisms can only be performed on mature adults.

418.   In a 2021 survey, Canadians revealed that firefighters were among the most respected professionals.

419.   In the same survey, Car Salespeople ranked 2nd from the bottom, lower than the elected members of Canada's parliament.

420.   In the town of Szymbark, Poland; there is a house that was built in 2007 that was upside down.

421.   The SnuzNLuz alarm clock is an alarm clock that connects via your Wi-Fi and every time you press the snooze button, it donates money to a political party you hate.

422. Enigma Machines used by the German Navy during the Second World War had 60 septillion possible encryption combinations.

423. The color line was an unofficial rule in American baseball, that excluded players primarily African Americans from Major League Baseball until Jackie Robinson signed with the Brooklyn Dodgers for the 1946 season.

424. Up until the 19th century, the ampersand was considered the 27th letter of the alphabet.

425. Tanks in the First World War, had genders; the male tanks would be equipped with six-pound guns, whereas female tanks would only equip machine guns.

426. From December 2001 to January 2002, Argentina had four presidents.

427. Around 40% of the world's population is overweight.

428. According to a survey of American men & women in relationships; 50% of men wanted their female partner to lose weight.

429. In the same survey, 4% of men wanted their female partner to gain weight.

430. In 1873, the first commercially produced toothpaste was launched by Colgate and originally sold in jars.

431. 2013 was the year when smart phones outsold basic no-nonsense "dumb phones".

432. Indian citizens do not require a visa to visit Jamaica.

433. The average cost of a wedding cake in 2021 for British couples, was £310.

434. The 21st most popular name for baby girls in the U.S. in 1900, was Gladys.

435. The 21st most popular name for baby boys in the U.S. in 1900, was Roy.

436. The average man will spend a month of his life on shaving.

437. The Israeli Defense Force prohibits the growing of facial hair unless a special request form has been filed and approved.

438. In some parts of India, police officers are paid more if they grow a moustache.

439. The average age that children stop believing in Santa Claus/Father Christmas is 8.

440. One third of job applicants lie about their references on their CV.

441. A CV or Curriculum vitae by definition includes a person's academic qualifications, achievements, skills, and experience as well as a summary of your work history; compared to a Résumé that is much shorter and primarily lists previous work history.

442. In computing, a "cookie" is a packet of data that software receives and sends back to a user; the term originates from a "magic cookie" and that term derives from a "fortune cookie".

443. When fortune cookies were originally invented, they were consumed with Tea.

444. Cheddar cheese comes from the village of Cheddar, Somerset; the product does not have a protected designation of origin due to the mass production across the world.

445. At 5 million tons annually, the world's largest producer of cheese is the U.S.

446. Four of Jesus' twelve apostles were fishermen.

447. Several Caribbean nations ban civilians from wearing camouflage.

448. The price of a first class ticket on the Titanic was around £30.

449. 100 years, that same ticket according to Bank of England inflation rates would equate to £2,060.20.

450. 20 people were reported to have canceled their plan to board the Titanic after having a dream that it would sink.

451. Evidence has been shown that Ancient Egyptians styled hair using a fat based gel.

452. Earth's most isolated tree, was destroyed in 1973 by a suspected drunk driver in Niger; it was an acacia and the nearest tree at the time was 250 miles away.

453. The name of the Ouija board derives from a word spelled out on the board when its inventor asked a ghost to name it.

454. In the U.S., January 15th is national hat day.

455. The UK counterpart 'Wear A Hat Day' is observed on the last Friday in March.

456. In 1981, Rajan Mahadevan accurately and correctly recited 31,811 digits of pi from memory.

457. Tekken 3 is the 5th best selling video game on the Sony Playstation.

458. Markus Persson, also known as 'Notch' is the creator of the Minecraft video game and was born on a Friday.

459. In Minecraft, when Notch's avatar dies; he drops an apple, making him the only player in the whole of Minecraft to have this feature.

460. Sugar doesn't spoil.

461. In 1533, King Henry VIII made hemp cultivation compulsory mandating that farmers had to use a certain proportion of land to grow hemp.

462. Up until very recently, squids, octopuses, and cuttlefish were believed to have been deaf.

463. The word Brother is mentioned 252 times in the King James version of the Old Testament of the Holy Bible.

464. In sailing, the term 'sheet' is a rope used to control the sail.

465. "Yellow journalism" is defined as a news source that presents little to no legitimate evidence or researched news while using exaggerated or content that evokes shock value to increase sales; an example of a publication that employs yellow journalism is the UK's Sunday Sport that mostly consists of topless females.

466. Doctor Martin Ellingham is the protagonist of the ITV medical drama series Doc Martin, created by TV producer Dominic Minghella; Dr. Ellingham was

named as such as it was an anagram of Minghella.

467. At 114 metres high, the ArcelorMittal Orbit is the tallest sculpture in the UK.

468. At 178 metres in length, the slide at the ArcelorMittal Orbit is home to the world's longest tunnel slide; it would take you 40 seconds to reach the bottom.

469. The world's longest water slide is 1,111 metres in Penang, Malaysia.

470. The original name of Mr. Monopoly is Rich Uncle Milburn Pennybags.

471. The infinity symbol or a horizontal figure of eight is known as a "lemniscate".

472. Due to a quirk of French copyright laws, the copyright for the Eiffel Tower expired in 1993, 70 years after the death of the original engineer, Gustave Eiffel.

473. Under the same law, the copyright for the night-time lights on the Eiffel Tower won't expire until at least 2055, as the lights are seen as a separate artistic creation.

474. U.S. patent 4,022,227 filed by Frank & Donald Smith in 1975, concerns a method of styling hair to cover partial baldness using only the hair on a person's head.

475. Ruine Liechtenstein are ruins of a castle that are based in Austria, not Liechtenstein.

476. The national anthems of the UK & Liechtenstein have the same melody.

477. In 1984, Liechtenstein held a referendum on women's suffrage; the referendum was only allowed to be voted on by males and the vote passed with 51.29% voting in favour of giving women the right to vote, this made Liechtenstein the last country in Europe to allow women to vote.

478. Guillaume Le Gentil was an astronomer who after an 2 unsuccessful attempts to observe the transits of Venus from India; returned to Paris after 11 years to find that he had been declared legally dead, his belongings had been plundered, he lost his seat in the Royal Academy of Sciences, and his wife had re-married.

479. Richey Edwards of the Manic Street Preachers, was declared legally dead on the 24th November 2008 after his disappearance in 1995; and for every live performance, the band set up an additional microphone in his honour.

480. Duo, West Virginia; is an unincorporated place 6 miles north-east of Quinwood.

481. The sign that welcomes tourists to Las Vegas, isn't legally in the city of Las Vegas, it sits in the unincorporated place of Paradise, Nevada.

482. In 1987, the U.S. first used DNA testing in the case of a Tommy Andrews who was accused of raping a woman during a burglary, Andrews was convicted because the defendant's DNA matched with the DNA that was collected from the crime scene.

483. The first usage of DNA fingerprinting in the UK, was in a police forensic test in 1986.

484. Faith Spotted Eagle is an activist and politician who is a member of the Sioux nation, she is one of two women to receive an electoral vote during a U.S. presidential election, the other is Hillary Clinton.

485. Faith Spotted Eagle is also the first native American/American Indian to receive an electoral vote for President of the U.S.

486. The daughter of Sargon of Akkad, Enheduanna was a high priestess of the moon god Nanna and is credited as the world's first author.

487. Presque vu is defined as the failure as remember something and you feel like you're about to say it, it's also known as "tip of the tongue".

488. The most common colour for toilet paper in France, is pink.

489. An average 31 year old would have spent 12 years of their life asleep.

490. AOL was the 2nd most visited website in the year 2000, 22 years later; it's the 177th most visited.

491. Out of the world's 50 most visited websites in December 2022, 5 websites are 'adult content'.

492. In 2016, it was estimated that 58.31% of all e-mail traffic was spam.

493. "Dermatoglyphics" and "Uncopyrightable" are the longest words in the English language that don't repeat any letters.

494. Levan Saginashvili has won the World Arm Wrestling Championship twice with his right hand and won the championship 5 consecutive times with his left hand.

495. On the 1st August 2021, Mutaz Essa Barshim of Qatar and Gianmarco Tamberi of Italy, shared the Olympic Gold medal for the high jump.

496. People who share are allergic to latex also have an increased allergy for avocados, bananas, kiwis, and tomatoes as these foods share similar proteins.

497. A researcher at Stanford University claimed that when you flip a coin, there is a natural bias and 51% of the time, the coin will land on the side that was facing up when it was flipped.

498. On a standard analog clock, the hour and minute hands will align 22 times in a 24 hour period which is roughly once every 65 minutes.

499. The first ever call from a mobile phone was on the 3rd April 1973.

500. And finally, smiling releases dopamine which is a neurotransmitter that releases antibodies from the brain that ultimately, improve our immune system.

Bonus Fact #1: You can buy the sequel to this book "Another 500 Useless Facts That Nobody Wanted To Know" available on Amazon and various other book retailers. (ISBN: 9798850051235)

Bonus Fact #2: I'd like to thank my best friend Louise for giving me encouragement on finishing this book.

Bonus Fact #3: This book is finished, you may now stop reading this page.

Printed in Great Britain
by Amazon

34534175R00046